The Top Bunk

By Cameron Macintosh

"We will go on a big trip in this van!" said Mum.

"It's pink!" yelled Saff.

"It's big like a tank!" said Hank.

Saff and Hank went
in the van.

"Bunk beds!" yelled Saff.

"I want that top bunk!" said Hank.

"You are too little for top bunks!" yelled Saff.

"I am **not**!" yelled Hank.

"What is all this fuss?"
said Dad.

"Saff will not let me have
the top bunk," said Hank.

Dad had a think.

"Test the top bunk with a quick nap, Hank," said Dad. "Then Saff can test it."

Hank got up on
the top bunk.

He had a **long** nap!

Hank got down off
the top bunk.

He fell!

"I got you!" said Saff.

"Thanks, Saff!" Hank said.

So Saff went up,
and Hank went down.

CHECKING FOR MEANING

1. Why did Saff say Hank couldn't sleep on the top bunk? *(Literal)*

2. What did Dad say Hank and Saff should do? *(Literal)*

3. Why do you think Hank liked it down on the bottom bunk? *(Inferential)*

EXTENDING VOCABULARY

bunk	Talk about the meaning of the word *bunk* in this story. A bunk bed is a set of beds stacked above each other.
test	What is the meaning of the word *test* in this book? Is there another meaning of this word? Can you use the other word in a sentence to show its meaning? E.g. I had a test at school today.
Thanks	*Thanks* is a shortened form of the words *thank you.* Explain that we say *thanks* more often in conversation, but use *thank you* in more formal settings.

MOVING BEYOND THE TEXT

1. If you have slept in bunk beds, how did you decide who slept on the top and bottom bunks?

2. Why do children usually want to sleep on the top bunk?

3. Can you think of things you aren't allowed to do because you are not old enough or big enough? Why do we have these rules?

4. What other way could Saff and Hank have decided who had the top and bottom bunks?

SPEED SOUNDS

ft	mp	nd	nk	st

PRACTICE WORDS

tank

pink

Hank

bunks

bunk

think

Thanks

and

Test

test